MW01483504

THE PARENT/CHILD MANUAL ON PEER PRESSURE

THE PARENT/CHILD MANUAL ON PEER PRESSURE

MARIA SULLIVAN

Illustrated by Chris Otsuki

TOR

A TOM DOHERTY ASSOCIATES BOOK
NEW YORK

THE PARENT/CHILD MANUAL ON PEER PRESSURE

Copyright © 1988 by RGA Publishing Group, Inc.

A TOR BOOK
Published by Tom Doherty Associates, Inc.
49 West 24 Street
New York, NY 10010

Library of Congress Cataloging-in-Publication Data

Sullivan, Maria.
    The parent/child manual on peer pressure / Maria Sullivan ;
    illustrated by Chris Otsuki.
        p. cm.
    1st ed.
    "A TOR book."
    Summary: Examines different kinds of peer pressure and gives clues
to parents on how to recognize them. Also assures children that being
independent and assertive will not cause them to lose friends.
    ISBN 0-312-93090-9 : $12.95
    1. Peer pressure—Juvenile literature. 2. Conformity—Juvenile
literature. [1. Peer Pressure. 2. Conformity. 3. Interpersonal relations.]
I. Title.
HQ784.P43S85 1988
303.3'27—dc19   88-19235
                                                            CIP

First edition: September 1988
0 9 8 7 6 5 4 3 2 1

ACKNOWLEDGMENTS

Many thanks for professional advice from Dr. Patricia Doyle, coauthor of *The Child in Crisis* (New York: McGraw-Hill, 1986), a Manhattan psychologist for twelve years.

I'm also grateful to Dr. Neville Kyle, clinical psychologist and Chief of Psychological Services with the Hacker Clinic in Lynwood and Los Angeles, California. Dr. Kyle has specialized in children's therapy for the past twenty-three years.

Thanks, finally, to RGA Communications.

Introduction

People can survive a few days without food or water. But put a human being into a sensory deprivation environment—without light, sound, or touch—and that person will soon ask to be released, usually within a couple of hours. Experiments have shown that even when subjects are offered increasing amounts of money to remain in a lightless, soundless enclosure, without human contact, they refuse, or soon emerge, forfeiting monetary reward to regain stimulation.

Without others we would be locked into a solitude that we couldn't face. The slogans about "going it alone" and "standing on our own two feet" aren't as pure as we'd like to think. People need each other!

So then how do we develop into strong, independent individuals? How can we dare to do or say things that might alienate us from our friends? How do we teach our children to deal with these issues? Most important of all, how do we teach our children that disagreeing with friends—even getting angry with friends or occasionally having a big fight—will *not* automatically end a relationship. Arguments and reconciliations are a big part of getting along with other people.

Children naturally attach themselves to peer groups. This is a healthy part of growing up. Adults do the same thing when they "network" or join clubs. There's nothing wrong with being influenced by friends. If Jimmy comes home and begs you to buy him the latest tennis shoes, it's not because he's giving in to "the crowd." When twelve-year-old Susan wants to wear lipstick, it doesn't mean that she's taking orders from some leader of the pack. It just means that they want to fit in and be liked. They're trying to figure out how to grow up. Don't assume that wanting to be like the others means that your child can be easily led into shoplifting; using drugs, cigarettes, or alcohol; or other destructive behavior.

Parents must teach their children how to say no or speak up when they feel pressured into doing something. If a big kid says to Jimmy, "I dare you to spray paint that wall with graffiti," and taunts him with "Chicken!" when he hesitates, how does Jimmy reconcile wanting that kid to like him with avoiding something he knows is wrong? Our children need to learn that saying no occasionally does not mean the end of a good friendship.

This *Parent/Child Manual on Peer Pressure* offers parents suggestions, anecdotes, and psychological insights that will help them steer their children into understanding that friendships can survive differences of action and opinion. As we will illustrate in this book, alternate groups of friends, an understanding atmosphere in the home, and good role modeling can help children deal with complex situations. Your kids can be strong individuals—and still have the confidence and warmth that comes from having good friends.

CHAPTER ONE

The Influence of the Peer Group

During the twenties and thirties, psychological thinking emphasized the mother-child relationship as the most vital part of a child's healthy emotional development. While no one would dispute how important the maternal (and paternal) bond is in turning an infant into a loving, well-adjusted adult, psychologists until recently discounted the substantial influence of the *peer group* upon the development of our children.

There are plenty of reasons for us to reconsider child-to-child friendships and outside-the-family peer pressures. Think of the incredible changes since World War I, which have affected not only the family structure, but the way children relate to parents. In addition to a rise in the divorce rate (in this decade about 45 percent of American children will have divorced parents), the family has surrendered more and more of its influence to secondary social factors, such as teachers, school authorities, police, counselors, etc.

The community-at-large is now required, sometimes by law, to assume a much bigger role in caring for children. If Johnny gets beaten up at school, the first friendly face he can turn to is probably a counselor or teacher. Parents are not his only resource.

Boys and girls are bombarded with a wide variety of options

and opinions about what it means to be male or female in our society. Throw in the tremendous population explosion—perhaps two-thirds of all the humans ever born are alive today—and it's no wonder confusion reigns! It's tough for kids to know where to turn.

As parenting tasks shift to outside the family, kids need the reassurance of "secondary families." Bonding with their peers, whether in the Scouts, the science club, or an after-school counseling group, can provide children with much-needed comfort and a sense that they are not alone.

A *peer,* by the way, is merely a friend, someone in the child's social circle. *Peer pressure* is the influence our friends have on us. The vast majority of this is not bad! Our friends can

affect what we wear or what games we play, and there's nothing wrong with that. It's only when peer pressure tries to push us into things we don't want to do that it becomes a problem.

Many parents make the mistake of thinking that a child's desire to form support groups outside the home signals weakness or a lack of independence. Not true! Kids need all the friends they can get. Little Johnny probably will feel a lot safer from that bully if he has a circle of friends and allies—an island of safety and support in an often hostile world. This doesn't mean that he can't defend himself; it means that he can be more confident and unafraid because he knows he has peers who care about him.

"Each person starts out with no advance data, other than a few instincts, on what it means to be alive in the world," says Dr. Neville Kyle, a Los Angeles-based psychologist who has specialized in children's therapy for twenty-three years. Many of our discoveries about being alive come through our relationships with others.

For instance: Johnny sees that his friends are concerned enough about him to discourage the bully from waylaying him.

He learns that although growing up has many hazards, a peer group will watch out for him and protect him. This in turn makes him want to look out for those peers.

When Sally is upset about her parents' divorce, she knows that the other children of divorce in her after-school counseling group can offer advice and comfort by sharing their own similar stories. She learns not only that pain is a terrible but unavoidable part of growing up, but that no matter how bad it seems, she is not alone.

Another crucial point: Single, close relationships do not entirely compensate for a lack of a group identity or network. Adults seek club activities to widen their friendship circles; successful businesspeople seek out new contacts. Human beings are social animals who must operate within larger spheres of influence.

The bigger and more varied are our children's peer groups, the more likely they are to grow up confident about their places in the world. If Doreen is encouraged to play softball with the boys in her neighborhood and to invite them to her parties, she's likely to grow up seeing boys as people, not as "them." In fact, studies of businesspeople demonstrate that men and women who have the fewest troubles with the opposite sex had both boys and girls as childhood friends.

Doreen's friendships with some of the Hispanic and Black children in her class also give her a chance to see that intelligence and human needs are not culture- or race-determined. Because Doreen has dinner at these friends' houses and shares her secrets with them, she realizes that similarities and not differences are what bind people together. The result? Doreen is more at ease in dealing with people who are different from her. She avoids the *polarization,* or Them-Us thinking, that plagues so many of us. These peer pressures in Doreen's life are very helpful!

There's another side to peer pressure, unfortunately. Insecure or vulnerable children may be swayed to do what a peer

tells them, even when it is obviously wrong. If ten-year-old Jason has just moved into the neighborhood and will do anything to stop feeling lonely, he might not have enough self-esteem to refuse when one of the popular kids asks him to play a mean trick on Old Man Rodriguez. Negative peer pressure is not always applied to drugs, alcohol, or sexual behavior, although those are some obvious temptations. Lying, cheating, stealing, or leaving someone "different" out of a game are also ways a peer group might steer a child wrong.

It isn't always the new or lonely kid who is vulnerable. Sometimes children are more afraid to lose their old friends, because they can't imagine life without them. It can be harder to disagree with or say no to a familiar face than a new one.

Take the case of Dennis, whose best friend, Alex, asked for help in cheating on the history exam. Because he gets along so well with Alex, Dennis has a much bigger conflict than if some new kid in town had made the same request.

If there is a loving environment at home, Dennis will feel comfortable about discussing this problem with one or both of his parents. He knows that his parents won't judge him or belittle his feelings of crisis. This is what might happen:

DENNIS: Alex wants me to sneak him the answers to Mr. Wong's history test tomorrow. He's afraid he won't pass.

DAD: Oh? That sure puts you on the spot.

DENNIS: Yeah. I don't want to do it, but I don't want him to flunk.

DAD: I can understand that. Cheating will make you feel terrible, though, won't it?

DENNIS: Right. But Alex will get pretty mad if I don't help him. I don't know what to do.

DAD: How about if you promise to help him study for the test? That way you're being a good friend, but you're not doing something you know is wrong.

DENNIS: You think he'll go for that?

DAD: Sure. And you know what? If he knows that this is your position, the next time he probably won't put you on the spot.

DENNIS: Thanks, Dad. I'll go call Alex right now.

Because Dennis's dad showed him that he could say no to Alex and still be his friend, Dennis felt confident about standing up for what he knew was right. Saying no to Alex didn't mean the end of their long friendship. If anything, it strengthened the bonds of mutual respect between them!

CHAPTER TWO

When to Say Yes

How to "Give In" Gracefully

It's a funny paradox that in their drive to be different, children often want to look exactly like their peers. Parents don't understand how a child's "I want to be my own person!" translates so easily into "I want to be like everyone else my age!" Parents can't figure out where this collective desire for a faddish hair style, popular running shoes, or loud radios comes from.

According to Dr. Patricia Doyle, coauthor of *The Child in Crisis* (McGraw-Hill, 1986) and a Manhattan psychologist who has treated many young adults, teenagers, and children, this shift away from parents and toward peers is a normal part of growing up. "When we're dealing with issues of separation and individuation," she says, "other people and groups can provide security in transition. Six-year-olds going off to school begin to separate from the family. By the time they are teenagers, they are not only leaving the family but are concerned with identity formation."

According to Doyle, parents can't expect kids to go into the world without seeking the supportive atmosphere that groups can provide. Because children are simultaneously trying to figure out how they are different from their parents while seeking the love and understanding of new peers, they often adopt the emblems or ways of thinking of those peers. A child's identity can borrow heavily from outside influences.

Parents should not take this as a rejection. Instead, they should see their child's growing pains for what they are: an attempt by a child to figure out how to fit in and still be an individual—not a carbon-copy of Mom and Dad, not a pushover to his or her peers. Unfortunately, parents often clamp down on their kids' desires to be like their pals, figuring that the little things are the small rocks that could lead to a rebellious avalanche.

According to many psychologists, nothing could be further from the truth. Parents are often urged to let children have a few small things. Haircuts and clothing are *not* the issue. Maybe those bangs in Henry's face are driving you crazy. You can't understand how he can see, much less why he thinks that style is attractive. But why make hairstyle into a big issue? Why set up such a silly roadblock for communicating with Henry? Those bangs do not mean he is one step away from drug use or disaster. But if you keep after him about them—and other aspects of his appearance—you may be cutting off the important lines of communication that you'll need for things that really matter.

If your son Bob wants to wear glittery sneakers like the other boys in his class, it does not mean that he isn't his own person. Having that superficial equipment could make Bob feel more secure in his peer group and in a better position to speak his mind. Bob has a good opinion of himself. Those sneakers look pretty sharp, and that makes him happy. By his parents' standard, he's no fashion plate, but he looks all right and people like him. Bob doesn't feel isolated and doesn't have to scheme his way into the group.

We're not recommending that you rush out and buy your children all the latest fashions. Children should also learn about frugality and common sense. They should understand the value of money and should be encouraged to establish a personal sense of taste. Who a person is inside is more important than what he or she looks like, and no amount of fashionable dressing will guarantee that an insecure child becomes confident. Neverthe-

less, the point remains: Don't make external trappings the central issue!

Allowing your child a few sought-after trinkets, or accepting what is to you a strange haircut, can open the way for a more important lesson: Wanting to be like the other kids is O.K. when it's harmless. Agree on the small stuff so that you and your child can pave the way for a discussion of the more important aspects of peer pressure.

Indicate to your children that you want them to be happy, that you're willing to meet them halfway on little things, and you are well on your way toward establishing an atmosphere of acceptance and communication. Since dinnertime at Henry's house stopped being one big fight about his hair, Henry has felt more relaxed and has told his Mom and Dad about more of the things going on at school. And ever since Bob found those special sneakers at the breakfast table for his birthday, he's begun to think that his parents really are on his side.

Forget About Lecturing

It's tempting for parents to lecture their kids about what is good and bad for them. If the child is younger than nine, this might work. Young children are eager to please their parents. If asked why it isn't a good idea to pick on a smaller kid, the child might reply, "Because Daddy told me not to."

Between the ages of about nine and eleven, children continue to respond to verbal warnings from authority figures, but by then they've developed ideas of their own. It isn't a good idea to pick on a smaller kid because they themselves don't think that's a nice thing to do.

Once the kids pass age eleven, however, the formulas that worked when they were younger go straight out the window. Many psychologists consider eleven as the beginning of the teenage years. These kids are dealing with new physical strength and agility, more outside resources, and the onset of sexual drive. Lecturing doesn't work, and neither does being rewarded for good behavior and punished for bad. Parents don't understand why they can't use the same old methods of discipline. "Because I said so!" may force a six-year-old to behave, but don't count on it being effective on a teenager.

Parents should clearly explain the boundaries of good behavior. A child of any age can understand your expectations.

Permissiveness, or letting children figure out the perimeters on their own, is not helpful. Children must know absolutely what is unacceptable, whether it's taking the canoe into deep water or smoking marijuana. When rules are established, the child knows exactly what you will find right and wrong.

All children respond to affectionate support and clear demonstrations that they are loved by their parents. Sadly, many parents are too inhibited to express their emotions, even though showing love is the best way to convince a child that he or she is lovable. This knowledge gives a child a powerful sense of self—the best possible defense against negative peer pressure.

Frequent hugs and kisses, rough-and-tumble games with the kids and the dog, quiet moments spent reading or talking, going together to a sporting event—there are countless ways to demonstrate to your children that they are important to you. Children who feel loved are far more likely to act confidently with their peers and to come to you with their problems.

CHAPTER THREE

Role Models

Using Actions, Not Words

It's much easier for a child to say no to something when he sees others saying no. *Positive modeling* can achieve more than all the parental lectures in the world. It's an old cliché, but actions speak louder than words.

The success of the "Scared Straight" program at New Jersey's Rahway Prison attests to this action-rather-than-words principle. Incorrigible teenagers, who'd had every possible threat leveled at them, did not demonstrate any desire to go straight until actual convicts gave them the sight, sounds, and taste of where they were headed. The scare tactic worked because it had an immediate effect. It was not simply a lecture.

Peer Modeling doesn't have to be that scary or striking. Your child is probably not a hardened incorrigible on the way to heavy drug use. But what about Ben, an eight-year-old who threw rocks at a child with Down's syndrome because some other kids dared him to do it?

Ben's mother had a good solution. She was furious and ashamed with what Ben had done, and she punished him by sending him to his room. She wanted it to be clear to Ben that she would not tolerate such actions. Later, she decided to ask him why he'd been so cruel.

MOM: You don't look too happy. Do you feel bad about hurting Joseph?

BEN: I guess so.

MOM: Why did you throw rocks at him?

BEN: I don't know. Doug and Alan dared me to.

MOM: Why would they do that?

BEN: Joseph was staring at us. I think he wanted to play football with us.

MOM: Is that so terrible?

BEN: He gives me the creeps.

MOM: Ben, sometimes we don't know how to deal with people who are different. Joseph was born with a problem. His body is growing, but his mind is still like a child's. But everyone, including Joseph, wants to be liked.

BEN: Well, Doug and Alan don't like him either. What was I supposed to do?

Ben's mother explained a few things that the boys might do to make Joseph feel like part of the group. She also thought of something she could do that would help Ben realize that Joseph was a person just like he. Since she was a physical therapist, one day she took Ben to the hospital where she worked. Ben's mother was treating a young boy named Christopher who had Down's syndrome and physical disabilities. She was teaching Christopher how to walk, and she let Ben watch a lesson. She also showed Ben how much Christopher liked to play catch.

She was smart enough to realize that her son had been cruel to Joseph more out of fear and ignorance than out of malice. Once she "demystified" mental and physical disabilities for her son and showed him how good it felt to help Christopher, she thought he might be more understanding about dealing with disabled people. By being a good role model, she *showed* rather than just *told* Ben what to do. Next time his peers said mean

things about Joseph, Ben would feel stronger about standing up to them. He might even try playing catch with Joseph, so he wouldn't feel so left out.

Ben's mother was in a great position to give her son positive role modeling, but what if you want your children to avoid something you indulge in? If you smoke, it's much harder to convince your children that they shouldn't. Instead of a meaningless "You shouldn't smoke because I said so!" lecture, consider the conversation Jeanine had with her mother:

> JEANINE: Why can't I smoke? You do! You're a regular chimney!
>
> MOM: I know it. I've tried to stop a hundred times. If I could turn back the clock to your age, I

would never have started. There are so many horrible things that smoking can do to our health!

JEANINE: I just want to smoke for a few years. Then I'll quit.

MOM: It's not that easy! You can see how tough it is for me to stop. Smoking is very, very addictive.

JEANINE: A lot of the girls at school are doing it.

MOM: I bet there are a lot more girls and boys at school who aren't. Smoking is something I'm struggling with, and I'd hate to see you make the same mistake I did!

JEANINE: You must enjoy it, because you keep doing it. So why can't I?

MOM: You know something? I don't enjoy it. That's the strange part. I hate the way it makes me feel. Maybe it's time I signed up for one of those stop smoking programs. Does that sound like a good idea? You and Dad and Marty are probably sick of breathing the polluted air in this house!

Obviously, Jeanine's mother will be in a stronger position to convince her daughter not to smoke if she gives up cigarettes. Psychologists point out that even young children can see through the flimsy "smoke screen" of empty talk—why not choose this opportunity to back up your words with action? That will convince your children that getting help when necessary and making the commitment to fight a bad habit is a worthwhile struggle. Enlist their help in keeping you straight—that will make them feel more adult.

No one is perfect, and it never hurts to show that you're only human. After all, your kids want to feel that if they slip up, they can still talk to you. By fostering a nonjudgmental atmosphere, you'll encourage children to be more open about their worries and mistakes. Children often want advice about their foul-ups, but they'll keep mum if they think that talking about their mistakes will always lead to a punishment or a lecture. Let them know that you're there for them—and that you realize they're only human, too!

CHAPTER FOUR

Creating an Open Atmosphere

Shared Activities

No amount of assertiveness or social-skills training can replace the powerful effects of love. Obvious affection from a parent—including supportive touching, hugging, and shared activities—works miracles in building a child's self-esteem. This is the key to developing a strong personality. A child with a good sense of self knows that he or she can speak up, even disagree with his or her friends, and that the world will not collapse, that he or she will not be deserted by those friends.

A child who wonders if he or she is loved by his or her parents might develop a pattern of "trying to please" that could manifest in a negative way to a peer situation. Such a child is in a vulnerable position, willing to do anything for a sign of approval from somebody.

Parents should recognize that societal change has put an increasing load of parental responsibility on outside sources. Many parents assume that these secondary groups are taking care of their children's emotional needs. *Take back some responsibility through scheduled, shared activities.* Not only will it demonstrate your love for your children, it will encourage them to trust you.

As your child grows up and seeks affection from peers and those outside the family, family-shared activities will naturally diminish. The parent-child relationship evolves into a loving distance that acknowledges how all of you are changing. Your interests may diverge, and you may not always have time for each other.

You may not get to take Matthew fishing every weekend, but why not support his new interest in painting by taking him to the County Museum once a month? Matthew will learn that you respect his desire to be with his friends and that it's important to plan some activities in advance. But that doesn't mean you don't need each other anymore. Show that you still have fun with him, love him, and want to be a part of his life.

A Chance to Win

Children who feel good about themselves are better equipped to resist going along with the crowd when necessary. They'll also have a sense that the friend they just argued with still wants to be their friend. A little girl who's applauded for her beautiful piano playing has positive approval in her life. She doesn't care about the approval of the girls who drink in the park; she has plenty of musician friends who love her and share her interests.

Of course, life isn't that simple. The boy who won the science prize at the fair will still suffer when his classmates taunt him because he can't slide into home base. In fact, some kids may tease him over his "brains" too. But at least he knows that he excels in a particular area, and that some people admire what he's done and want to be his friends. He may not win "Most Popular"—but he's won something else that's equally valuable.

Help your child find an area where he or she can shine.

Everyone has at least one. If your child displays an obvious talent in music, dance, singing, or sports, that's fine. But excellence does not have to be grandiose. Does your child have a way with animals or a green thumb? Is your son or daughter a great babysitter? Can he or she tell a joke that makes everybody laugh? Give him or her a chance to use those abilities. If your child does not seem to manifest any particular talent, you may have to dig a bit, but there is no one who does not have some latent gift.

Children who feel good about their accomplishments, learn that they are worthwhile people. They have something to contribute! That kind of self-confidence can go a long way toward making children feel secure about speaking up for what they believe in. This security helps them feel comfortable with their friends, able to disagree or suggest alternative activities now and then without changing the basic structure of a friendship. Besides, uncovering ways for your children to win can lead them to expanded peer groups with similar, healthy interests!

Create Alternatives

Teach your children that one source of approval is not all that counts. Point out that there are many different types of people, who can offer us a variety of experiences, emotions, and friendship.

Barbara had one close friend, Eliza, who often went away for the summer. Barbara was terribly lonely when Eliza left and began hanging around with a tough gang of girls just because she had no idea what to do or where to fit in—and these girls had plenty of suggestions! Barbara didn't have to make any decisions on her own.

Barbara's parents suggested that she join a swimming camp in the morning and attend a crafts class at the local art center during the afternoons. Life couldn't grind to a halt whenever Eliza went away! Barbara met a number of new boys and girls who shared her experiences. She was exposed to athletic and artistic children—and plenty who weren't very skilled but sure were having a good time. Having people to turn to—peers she could see even after Eliza returned at the end of summer—made Barbara feel much less alone or deserted.

Disagreements with one friend or group of friends is not nearly as painful for children who know that they can go elsewhere. They are more likely to say no to bad peer pressure if they can seek out other groups or allies. Barbara found it easier to refuse to hang around the mall, smoking cigarettes and shoplifting with the tough girls, because she knew that her swimming friends could suggest things that were a lot more fun to do.

Encourage Mixed Peer Dealings

Studies have shown that children often pick up clues about which peers to have from their parents. When two mothers like each other, for instance, the kids tend to gravitate toward each other. By guiding your children toward making friends with many different types of youngsters, you automatically broaden their thinking about who is acceptable and who isn't. Break the myth that group solidarity should be based only upon similarities!

Dealing With Loss

Never discount or underestimate the terrible trauma that disagreeing with a friend could be for your children. They might have said no to a bully or a creep, but it's still distressing to be rejected or taunted. When this rejection comes from a disagreement with a true friend, the result is doubly painful.

Many children will cave in to peer pressure to avoid this pain. It's not only that they don't want to be called a baby or a chicken. They're also confronting loss. Groups tend toward homogenity, and any disruption threatens the security and familiarity of the alliance. Your child is dealing with very real separation pangs when a disagreement over what is right and wrong threatens the group bond.

It's important to emphasize "It's O.K. to do and say different things and still stay friends with someone." Console your child by pointing out that real friendship and intimacy is based upon honest give-and-take. Sadly, that can involve some arguments and hurt feelings, but ultimately friends who really care about each other will reconcile, and they will gain a better understanding of the other's point of view. Disagreements are part of being human. Play up the positive aspects of disagreements with your children, and help them understand their friends' motives. Children who question why a friend thinks the way he or she does will feel much more in control of the situation.

When peers are engaged in something that is definitely wrong, such as smoking, drinking, taking drugs, stealing, lying, or sexual behavior beyond what the child can handle, disagreeing with them is not enough. It's necessary to take a "tough love" stance with these friends: they must give up the harmful activity and stop pressuring everyone into bad habits.

If you've taught your children to develop alternative groups of friends and other support systems, help them see that they have other peers who will not make them uncomfortable about standing up for what is right.

Walking Away, Telling Others

Let's say you've created an atmosphere in which your children can discuss his or her mistakes or the problems he or she faces at school or play. You've helped your child develop a sense of excellence and love and a network of options. They will still be reluctant to "fink" on their pals. Children feel all sorts of conflict at seeing their schoolmates doing things that are harmful.

Do not automatically alienate your child by bad-mouthing a "lousy punk." Your child's loyalty will be torn, and he or she might feel compelled to protect his or her friend. Instead, encourage your child to wonder *why* Amy thinks shoplifting is a thrill. Ask him or her to complete the sentence: "I think Amy does that because . . ." This will help your child figure out exactly why Amy is doing something wrong, and why he or she shouldn't be involved.

A nurturing environment will encourage your children to talk about what they really want, as opposed to what their peer groups are encouraging them to do. Does Dorothy want to wear makeup because everyone in her class is doing it, or because some lipstick will make her feel prettier? Why does she think

she needs it? Does Jake want to take up karate because a friend dared him to, or because he really wants to learn? Exploring reasons can help children understand their personal motives, which can prevent them from blindly following peers.

Above all, assure your child that it's O.K. to need friends . . . and that human relationships are complicated and imperfect, but ultimately worth all the trouble because of the great rewards true love and friendship can bring.

CHAPTER FIVE

The Assertive Child

Keys for Parents

Your child must learn to speak up—whether it's to disagree with a friend or right a wrong—in certain social situations. This can range from saying no to an offer of drugs to refusing to tease the new kid in class. Here are some tips that will help you to guide your child in becoming more assertive.

- Urge your child to ask *why*. Tell your child not to simply accept *or* resist the demands of a peer, but to figure out why that friend wants him or her to do a certain thing. With clarity of thought comes clarity of words.

- Never underestimate what situation your child might find to be formidable. As casual an action as asking for something in a restaurant can be traumatic for certain children.

- Don't bully or belittle a shy child into "speaking up." That will only shove him or her further into his or her shell. Instead, offer quiet support and provide ways for him or her to excel. This will build self-confidence.[1]

[1] Dr. Mitch Golant with Bob Crane, *It's O.K. To Be Shy!* (New York: TOR Books, 1987).

- Set a good example. The easiest way for children to learn assertiveness is by watching parents (teachers or counselors) behaving assertively.

- Counseling or classes in assertiveness skills for either you or your child are probably available in your area. These might best be thought of as a last resort. Pushing children into assertiveness training is rarely necessary, but it may be a valuable tool in assisting certain children who have developmental problems. Inquire about such programs through the school system, community centers, or child-therapy clinics. Make certain that the emphasis is on learning how to speak one's mind, not on attaining popularity.

The Child's Social Life

The most straightforward social confrontation is the business transaction, which provides a good training ground for a child who needs to learn when it's necessary to speak up—and how to handle such situations.

Here's an example:

SETTING: A soda parlor.

PARTICIPANTS: Carrie and her father. Carrie ordered a chocolate milk shake but was given strawberry.

FATHER: Carrie! I thought you ordered chocolate.

CARRIE: I did. I don't know why she gave me strawberry.

FATHER: I guess she made a mistake. I'll bet if you took that strawberry shake up to the counter, the girl would be happy to give you what you ordered.

CARRIE: But you already paid for this.

FATHER: That's O.K. You didn't get what you asked for, so you can take it back.

CARRIE: What if she doesn't remember me?

FATHER: Then you can remind her. It was only a short time ago. How about if I go with you?

CARRIE: Well—I can try it myself.

FATHER: O.K., but if you need me, I'll come right up.

Carrie's father does not belittle his child's hesitancy about what to him is a very simple transaction. He talks it through with Carrie and offers his support. He knows that his daughter is reasonably outgoing, and that this will be a practical, not traumatic, lesson for her. She's not afraid to go up to the counter herself; she's just a little uncertain of what the transaction will involve.

If Carrie was shy, however, it would be unfair to put her under such pressure to perform. Her father would then have taken a more active role, stating that since a mistake had been made, he would go back to the counter and get it fixed. This would show a shy child how to handle such a situation—without the gut-wrenching pressure of undertaking it before she felt ready. Don't set up win-loss contests or tests for your children or bludgeon them with assertiveness lessons. Everyone develops differently. Let their personalities be your guide.

Let's look at another child's assertiveness style.

SETTING: A barber shop.

PARTICIPANTS: Alex and the barber. Alex wants one of the popular "short on the sides, long on top" styles, but the barber wants to give him a crew cut.

ALEX: Hi, Mr. Mitchell. Can I have my hair trimmed on the sides and left long on top?

MR. MITCHELL: Why do you want to do that? It will look silly.

ALEX: Maybe. But that's what I want to try, please. My mother said I could have whatever style I wanted.

MR. MITCHELL: Why don't you want something short and sweet? How about if I just cut it off all the way around?

ALEX: No, thanks. I want it trimmed on the sides and left long on top.

MR. MITCHELL: If it's short all over, you won't have to come back as often. Why not save your mother some money?

ALEX: My mother said I could have the style I wanted, and I'd like my hair cut long on top and short on the sides, please.

MR. MITCHELL: You'll look like all those bums your age!

ALEX: That's O.K. It's what I want.

MR. MITCHELL: If you say so. It's your head.

Alex refused to be pressured into something he didn't want. He did not get nasty, but he remained firm. He made sure that Mr. Mitchell would respect his wishes and not turn his head into a disaster. Mr. Mitchell's line, "Why not save your mother some money?" was a guilt technique that Alex would not be drawn into. Alex had learned how to keep his own opinion without wavering and had applied *repetition* to the situation. The child who is taught to keep insisting, in a clear, controlled voice, on what he or she wants will eventually break down the peer (or authority) pressure.

Alex never raised his voice or got sidetracked into an argument about which hairstyles are good and which are old-fashioned.

Repetition is not simply saying no over and over. A parrotlike, needle-stuck-in-one-place response is likely to elicit even more derision from a pressuring peer. Teach your children the techniques of (1) insistence, (2) quiet reasoning, (3) alternative suggestion, and (4) repetition—all backed up by action.

FOR INSTANCE: Zeke wants John to share some wine with him.

JOHN: No, thanks. I don't want to drink.

ZEKE: Come on. What's the big deal?

JOHN (Insistence): No, I really don't want to.

ZEKE: Why are you being such a wimp?

JOHN (Quiet Reasoning): There are a lot of things I'd rather do. Drinking is something I'd rather not even start.

ZEKE: Well, I'm going to have some. You're being a total jerk.

JOHN (Alternative Suggestion): It'd be a lot more fun to play some of my brother's new tape cassettes. He said I could use them anytime. Wanna come along?

ZEKE: Let's have some wine first.

JOHN (Action): No. I'm going home, Zeke. You can come if you want. (Walks off.)

John held his ground firmly, without saying no, no, no over and over—although that was definitely the content of each message he gave his friend.

These social skills will help your children resist the toughest scenario of all: negative peer pressure from friends.

By the time your children are in junior high, they have been exposed to social dares, drugs, smoking, and alcohol, among other temptations. Let's look at one that's especially tough because it's so prevalent in our society: alcohol. Many adults drink. Alcohol is featured prominently in the entertainment media and in advertisements. Liquor stores abound. How can children learn to say no to something to which society obviously says yes?

The first solution would be for parents to limit their own drinking. Still, children can face heavy pressure from peers on this issue.

Eleanor does not want to drink, but her friend Sandy has taken a bottle of vodka out of her parent's cocktail bar. Instead of painting posters for the school Oktoberfest, Sandy wants to have a few drinks.

SANDY: Let's have a few!

ELEANOR: No thanks, Sandy. We've got these posters to finish.

SANDY: A few drinks will help us finish.

ELEANOR: No thanks. Vodka will make us sick.

SANDY: Sick? What're you talking about? My Dad has a drink every day when he comes home from work! He says it helps him think.

ELEANOR: That's fine, but I don't want any.

SANDY: Don't be such a nerd! Just have one.

ELEANOR: No thanks. Why do you want to drink?

SANDY: What do you mean "why"? Why not?

ELEANOR: Wouldn't you rather finish these posters? We can have a good time without the vodka. It would make me much happier if you didn't drink.

SANDY: Everybody drinks.

ELEANOR: No, they don't. *I* don't!

SANDY: O.K., you win.

Eleanor's insistent no—good use of repetition—was helped when she asked why Sandy wanted to drink. She came up with plenty of quick reasoning (saying no in a different way), and she suggested alternative activities. Sandy had to confront—probably for the first time—that her desire for alcohol was based on knee-jerk impulse. "Everybody drinks" was the only reason she thought she had to do it, too!

Instead of harping on "your parents will find us," or "your parents will punish us," Eleanor kept authorities out of the issue and directed matters solely toward herself and her friend. She did not assume a "holier-than-thou" attitude, and she made it clear, in an assertive but friendly way, that she would not stand for drinking. Far from losing a friend, she strengthened the friendship.

These scenarios are, of course, highly idealized. Carrie, Alex, and Eleanor are mature and articulate, and they are confident in social transactions. As we all know, learning to speak up or disagree with a friend isn't always so easy. But your children can see by these and other examples that speaking up doesn't always mean the loss of friends or being left alone. Staying reasonable and coming up with alternatives—and walking away when that's absolutely necessary—can open up whole new worlds of personal integrity and self-respect, and strengthen the bonds of friendship.

CHAPTER SIX

Read the following stories aloud with your children. They deal with one of the toughest trials children face: how to say no when group pressure is forcing them to do something wrong. Sometimes it's more complicated than turning down an invitation to take drugs or alcohol. The crowd can attempt to persuade your child to do many things that make him or her uncomfortable, including poking fun at an unpopular child, lying, stealing, playing a practical joke on someone, or experimenting with sexual activities.

Select the stories that apply best to your child's needs; keep reading only as long as he or she is truly interested. These stories can be used to open a discussion with your child and to reassure the child that you care.

Explain to your children how to use the techniques of insistence, quiet reasoning, alternative suggestions, and repetition—reinforced by action. Emphasize that disagreeing with friends does not mean that friendships will be lost.

The children in these stories all react correctly—they disagree with friends rather than doing something they think is wrong. In the real world, no one can respond perfectly every time, but we hope these stories will show your child that speaking up when necessary won't destroy the world. Instead, it will open up entirely new avenues.

Doreen's Story

Doreen wanted to be as popular as Clara. They were both in the fifth grade. Doreen studied the way Clara dressed, walked, laughed, and even the way she chewed her pencil in class. Clara always had beautiful ribbons and pretty dresses, and Doreen wanted to be exactly like her.

Clara started an after-school club. She declared that to belong in the club, the girls had to wear cowgirl boots and miniskirts. Everyone wanted to do exactly what Clara said, but Doreen was worried. She knew that cowgirl boots were expensive.

That night she talked to her mother about her problem.

"Why do you think Clara wants the girls to wear clothes like that?" said her Mom.

Doreen wasn't sure. "Because she's the boss, I guess."

"Do you think if you don't wear those clothes, you won't be in the club?" asked her Mom.

"Yes," Doreen said. "All the other girls are going to wear them."

"What kind of club is it?"

Doreen hadn't thought about that. "I don't know. I guess the girls will sit around and talk." Saying that didn't make the club sound very interesting. Doreen knew that she really wanted to join the club so that she could get to know Clara better.

"If it's important to you, Doreen, maybe we can figure out some jobs you can do to earn the money," said Doreen's

Mom. "Those boots cost more than I have in the budget right now."

Doreen knew how hard her mother worked to support her and her two brothers. Suddenly what Clara was asking didn't seem fair. "Actually, Mom, I don't care about the clothes," she said. "I only want them to be part of that club and be Clara's friend."

"Then why don't you invite her to go skating with you some Saturday? She may be a nice dresser, but I'll bet she doesn't know what a terrific ice skater you are! Tell her that you'll give her a lesson. Do you want your friendships to depend on what clothes you wear?"

Doreen knew that Victoria, Luisa, and a few of the other girls couldn't afford miniskirts and boots either. Not everyone would be in the club!

"Mom, I think you had a great idea. I'll ask Clara if she'll go ice-skating with me. If she won't, I'll bet some of the other girls in my class would love to!" Doreen was glad she'd talked to her Mom, because it helped her to see that she wanted friends who would like her for more than her clothes.

Have you ever wanted to be part of a special group? What did you do?

Eduardo's Story

One Saturday afternoon Eduardo and some boys from school were playing baseball. Eduardo was ten, but his friends were all ages—some younger and some older—already in junior high. When the game was over, Paul, one of the older boys, said, "Let's go see *The Demon's Nightmare.* It's playing over at the Coronet Theater. Old Man Correira sells tickets on the weekends, and he never checks IDs. Anybody with the money can get in!"

Eduardo had heard about this movie. It was supposed to be extremely scary and violent. Eduardo did not like horror films at all! They gave him nightmares. All the other boys seemed to go along with Paul's idea, but Eduardo did not want to join them.

"I'd rather not," he said. "I don't like horror movies."

Paul laughed. "Brawk! Brawk!" he shouted, making a chicken noise and flapping his arms like wings. "Come on, Eduardo!"

"Why don't we see something else? I think there's a sports movie playing at the Carlisle," Eduardo said. Eduardo remembered what his father had taught him about disagreeing with friends: If saying no in a quiet but firm way doesn't work, come up with other suggestions.

"Come on, Eduardo," said Jacob. "A scary movie won't kill you."

"What're you afraid of?" said Paul. "Let's go."

Eduardo remembered that his father also told him that sometimes it's best to walk away. If he kept standing there, saying no over and over, the boys would only laugh at him. He picked up his baseball mitt. "I'm going to that movie about the Olympics instead. Anyone who wants to join me is welcome," he said.

"The Olympics!" Jacob said. "That's a great idea. I'll go with you."

"Hey!" said Fernando. "That does sound like fun."

"You're all a bunch of chickens," said Paul, but he could see that the other boys had made up their minds.

Eduardo was glad that he had come up with another plan. Now he would have a good time sharing his love of sports with Jacob and Fernando. When he got home, he would tell his father how well everything had turned out.

What would you do if your friends wanted to do something you didn't want to do?

Eriko's
Story

Eleven-year-old Eriko was new in the neighborhood. She loved her parents, two sisters, and her brother. She got along very well with her grandparents, who lived close by. Despite this, she was lonely and wanted to have friends her own age.

Before long, she met some of the boys and girls on her block. Most of them went to the same school and had many things in common. Eriko always said hello, hoping that one day they'd invite her to join in some of their games or conversations.

One day a girl named Justine told Eriko that a few of the kids were going to have a really good time that afternoon, and she was welcome to come along.

Eriko was so excited and happy that she could hardly wait for school to let out. Then she discovered what the "fun" was: soaping the windows of an old man who lived on the street.

Eriko came from a cultural tradition in which older people were highly respected. She knew how she would feel if the kids did something like this to her grandparents. Eriko wanted friends, but if this was the price then she decided she would find some kids who had better ideas of fun.

"That man hasn't hurt anybody," Eriko said.

"So?" said Justine. "It's just for fun."

The other girls and boys started pressuring Eriko into playing this trick with them.

Eriko A

"No," said Eriko. She turned around and went home. She asked her mother and father to help think of ways for her to meet some new kids.

"How about if you sign up for that gymnastics class over at the community center?" suggested her father. "They're starting a special group for kids your age."

"That's a good idea," said her mother. "Or you could try out for the school band—I think a few of the girls in the band live in this neighborhood, and you like music."

How would you feel if somebody wanted you to play a mean trick on someone?

Bob's
Story

Bad things happened around Bob's house. His mother
and father fought all the time. They screamed and called
each other names. Bob's heart beat fast every dinnertime,
waiting for one of them to explode. Mostly they ignored Bob,
who was eleven, and his older brother, Tom, who was
sixteen. They drank beer until they got drunk enough to start
fighting again. That was only slightly better than the times
that Bob's Dad hit him for no reason.

Bob tried to get out of the house as much as possible.
He started hanging out on the corner with some boys who

sometimes stole wine from the liquor store. They taught Bob
how to do it. Bob would drink and steal with these boys as
often as he could.

One evening some smaller boys passed by, and Joel,
the gang leader, pushed one of them down. The little boy
cried out, but the gang members only laughed. They were all
a little drunk.

"Say 'uncle,' you little shrimp!" said Joel.

"Uncle!" yelled the boy.

Joel pretended not to hear. "I don't think that was loud
enough! Do you, boys?"

Bob couldn't believe what he was seeing. He'd had only
a little to drink that night, but it was making him sick to his
stomach. He felt horrible. Watching Joel and that little boy
was like watching his Dad picking on him! If he spoke up the

gang would turn on him, but Bob didn't care. He wasn't going to go along with the crowd.

"Knock it off," Bob told Joel.

"What did you say?" Joel asked.

"You heard me," said Bob. "If you're going to pick on a

kid, try someone your own size—like me!" He was shaking, but he didn't care.

To Bob's surprise, Joel let the little boy get up. Bob left the gang for good. Drinking and stealing had made him feel awful. He decided to talk to Mr. Perez, the school counselor. Mr. Perez might help him deal with what was happening at home.

How would you feel if you saw a big kid beating up a littler one?

Kim's Story

Twelve-year-old Kim loved to go shopping with her friends. The new mall in town had stores with shoes, jewelry, records, and miles and miles of clothing. There were more things to buy than anyone could ever imagine! Kim especially liked the mall during Christmas season. Then there was excitement in the air, and bright decorations hanging from the ceiling.

Kim had a problem when it came to Christmas shopping. There were so many pretty things she wanted to buy, for herself and her family, and she just didn't have enough money!

Her best friends, Joyce and Francesca, had a solution. "Everybody shoplifts, Kim," Joyce said when she noticed Kim gazing at a pink-and-blue bracelet on a department store counter. "Go ahead and take it. That saleswoman's back is turned."

"That's stealing!" said Kim. "I can't do that!"

"Don't be such a baby," said Francesca. "It's easy! I have my eye on that silk scarf over there."

"It's not really stealing, because they have so much stuff, and we only take little things. Who's it hurting, anyway?" said Joyce.

Kim's thoughts were whirling around. None of what her friends were saying made much sense. Stealing was stealing, no matter how many things were around. And stealing from a store and not a person didn't make it any less terrible! As for who it hurt, Kim had many answers: she would hurt her parents if she shoplifted, but most of all she would hurt herself. She would feel very bad about what she had done.

There were so many ways to enjoy life other than grabbing up a lot of things, Kim thought. She didn't need to own everything she saw and liked! They could go look at the puppies in the pet store, or toss some coins into the March of Dimes fountain to help children who were less fortunate.

"No," Kim told her friends. "I'm not going to steal, and I don't want to be around you if you do it, either."

"Oh, come on, Kim," said Joyce. "Are you serious?"

"Yes," said Kim. "There are lots of better things to do. Why don't we go get some ice cream instead?"

"She's right," Francesca said to Joyce. "Ice cream sounds a whole lot better than doing something terrible like shoplifting."

Kim was very glad that she'd disagreed with her friends and suggested something they could all share.

What would you do if one of your friends urged you to steal?

Pete's Story

Pete and his friends, who were all nine years old, often spent an hour after school playing basketball. One day a boy named Keith pulled out a package of cigarettes and wanted everyone to smoke before starting the game. Pete was sad to see a couple of his friends immediately reach for a cigarette.

Keith coughed as he held the cigarette pack out to Pete. "Go ahead," he said. "One won't kill you."

"It's O.K., Pete. It looks cool," Clarence said.

Pete didn't think it looked cool at all. His father smoked, and this upset Pete a great deal. His father had brown teeth and, even worse, couldn't climb the stairs at home without stopping to catch his breath. There was nothing "cool" about thinking his father was going to die young. Pete had begged his father to quit, but his Dad seemed completely addicted.

Now that doctors knew how much trouble smoking caused, it seemed incredibly dumb to start as a kid.

"Just have one," said Keith. "Don't be such a nerd, Pete."

Pete knew that "just one" could easily become two, three, and even more. If he smoked now, he would probably smoke again.

"No," he said. "I want to play basketball. I don't ever want to smoke." He felt terrific saying no like that, especially when two of the other boys instantly joined him in refusing to smoke.

Pete decided that that night, at home, he would talk to his Dad about smoking. He wanted to understand why his Dad did it, and why he couldn't stop.

Does anyone you know smoke? How does it make you feel?

Heidi's Story

Nine-year-old Heidi usually didn't mind doing her Saturday morning chores, but today was different. The Miramar theater was giving puppet shows all day long, and Heidi wanted to go with her friends to see the performance.

Even though she'd promised to finish her chores before walking over to Tommy Corcoran's house for a ride to the Miramar, Heidi wanted to quit. She didn't want to clean her room and wash the breakfast dishes. The garden needed weeding, and she had promised her Mom that she'd do that too. It would take forever! She was much too excited about the puppet show.

Tommy and Jobeth came over and tried to talk her out of doing her work. "Go talk to your mother," Jobeth said. "Tell her you're finished and want to go over to the Corcorans'."

They still had plenty of time to get to the theater. Heidi hesitated. She wanted to do exactly what her friends were telling her, but she hated lying to her Mom.

"I can't," she said.

"What's the big deal?" said Tommy. "I know we're early, but I want to get really good seats." He and Jobeth kept urging Heidi to lie.

"It's silly to lie when all I have to do is talk to my Mom," said Heidi.

She went in and found her mother taking care of the baby. "Mom, I have a problem," she said. "I know you want me to finish all my chores, but Jobeth and Tommy are already here. They want to leave early for the puppet show. I don't know what to do."

"Heidi, I don't want you to miss the puppet show. I know how much you've been looking forward to it. You can weed

the garden tomorrow. Why don't you give me a hand changing Ricky, and then you and your friends can walk over to Mrs. Corcoran's house."

Heidi thought her mother was great and gave her a hug. She was glad that she hadn't given in to Jobeth and Tommy and told her Mom a lie. It wasn't necessary, because her mother was always ready to listen to her.

What would you do?

Martin's Story

Luís was Martin's best friend. They were both eleven and had been buddies for a long time. They went swimming together and traded baseball cards during the summers and went to the movies during the winters. Whenever Martin wanted to get away from his three brothers and two sisters, he would go to Luís's house. Sometimes they would study together, and sometimes they would just have sodas and talk.

One night Martin went to a camp-out at Luís's house. A lot of boys from school were there, and after Luís's parents had gone to bed, Patrick pulled out a marijuana cigarette.

Patrick lit the joint and inhaled. "Have some," he said, handing it to Martin.

"Go on, Martin," said Luís.

Martin wanted Patrick to like him, and he did not want to make Luís mad. Luís might not speak to him again if he didn't smoke the joint.

But Martin thought dope was for dopes. All the boys were staring at him, and suddenly Martin got mad. He didn't like being put on the spot like this!

"No," he said, looking up at the stars in the sky. "I don't want any."

"Lighten up," Patrick said, taking back the marijuana.

"I can have plenty of fun without drugs," said Martin. He knew that the best way to say no was to walk away from people who were using something bad. "I guess I'll call my Mom to come get me," he said, standing up. Luís might get mad at him, but he wasn't going to smoke dope!

"Wait," said Luís, grabbing Martin's arm. "Patrick, put that out and throw it away. Martin's right!"

Martin was pleased that Luís was such a true friend. Sometimes it took moments like this to remind him that a real friend never wants to pressure someone into doing something that person doesn't want to do.

What would you do if someone offered you drugs?

Aurora's
Story

Aurora, who was eleven, was excited that Blue Dawn, one of her favorite bands, was giving a performance in her town. Aurora's mother had given her permission to go to the show with Mrs. Cheever and four other girls from her class. It would be a real party. Aurora couldn't believe how lucky she was!

The sports arena was crowded with all sorts of people, and everyone applauded when Blue Dawn started to play. The soft lights made the songs seem very romantic.

At intermission, Aurora and her friends headed for the ladies' room. Celeste, one of the girls, noticed that someone had left a purse near one of the sinks. "I'll bet it's got money in it!" she said. "Let's look."

There was about eighty dollars in the purse, and some jewelry—a gold chain and a pretty pair of earrings.

"We've struck it rich," said Celeste. "I'll take the chain and you can have the earrings, Aurora."

Aurora knew that the woman who'd forgotten her purse would be very upset.

"Hurry up," whispered Celeste. "The lady could be back any second. We have to act fast."

"There's a Lost and Found here," Aurora said. "If I'd lost something, I'd want someone to return it."

Celeste said, "Finders keepers, losers weepers."

"No," Aurora said, "it's stealing."

"It's not stealing," argued Celeste. "It's right out here in the open. If we don't take it, someone else will."

"I'll feel terrible, Celeste. I want to take it to the Lost and Found," said Aurora. She took the purse from Celeste and walked away. Celeste followed.

Just as Aurora handed the purse to an attendant at the Lost and Found, a woman came rushing up. "Oh, thank you, girls!" she said. "I've been frantic! The jewelry in there has big sentimental value for me. It was a gift for my tenth wedding anniversary. If I'd lost it, I'd be too upset to think

straight!" She reached into her purse and handed Celeste and Aurora each ten dollars.

"You don't need to pay us," said Aurora.

"I want to give you a reward for being honest," the woman said. "I can't thank you enough!"

Aurora enjoyed the rest of the concert, knowing that she had made someone happy. Celeste was happy about returning the purse, too. Seeing how glad the woman was was the best reward of all.

What would you do if you found something?

Keith's Story

Keith was doing very well in his seventh grade math class. His grades were good, and he studied hard. He wasn't sure what he wanted to be when he grew up, but he wanted math to be a part of it. Maybe he would be an engineer, or a scientist, or even a doctor.

One day, Keith and his friends Douglas, Corey, and Joshua were sharing soft drinks on their way home from school.

"If I don't pass that math test tomorrow, I'm in big trouble," said Douglas.

"Yeah," agreed Corey. "I haven't opened my book in a week! I've been too busy watching the basketball play-offs."

"I've got an idea!" said Joshua. "Keith, old pal, how about giving us a hand?" He, Corey, and Douglas laughed.

"In fact," Joshua said, "how about just giving us the answers?"

"What?" said Keith. He was surprised by Joshua's request. "I can't do that."

"Sure you can," Douglas said. "All you have to do is write down the answers on a paper and pass it to Joshua. He'll do the rest!" The boys laughed again.

Keith felt very uncomfortable. He knew that Corey and Douglas might flunk the test, and Joshua probably wouldn't do too well either. And if he didn't help them, his buddies might never speak to him again.

Keith wanted to run home and talk to his parents. They would help him figure this out. He wanted to hide in his room and pretend that this awful conversation wasn't happening.

But his friends kept pressuring him for an answer. "Come on, Keith!" Joshua said. "Are you going to be a friend, or not?"

Keith knew that if he helped them cheat, he would feel terrible. And what would keep them from asking him to cheat on the next test, and the next? Besides, math was important to Keith. Getting caught cheating would ruin all he had worked for.

He tried to think of a solution that would let him stand up for his rights and still make his friends feel good. "How about if I help you study? We can take an hour and go over the last chapter. I'm sure that's what Mr. Soares will test us on!"

"It'll be easier on us if you just pass us the answers," said Corey.

"But it'll be easier on me if I help you study. That's my final offer," said Keith.

Corey was mad, but Douglas and Joshua agreed that Keith was right. Keith was sorry that Corey felt angry, but he knew that Douglas and Joshua respected him for standing up for himself.

That night Keith talked to his Dad about what happened. His father said, "Don't worry about Corey, Keith. What you did was right. When Corey cools off, I'll bet he will respect you even more for not letting him push you around. And it was very generous of you to help the boys study!"

Keith agreed with his Dad. He was glad he'd disagreed with his friends' plan and come up with one of his own. The boys had studied hard. He hoped they would all pass.

What would you do if someone asked you to do something you didn't want to do?

Barbara's
Story

Barbara, who was twelve, liked having her friends visit.
Stan, Patricia, Debbie, Chrissy, and Orlando were all
rehearsing for the school play in Barbara's den. They were
drinking soft drinks and laughing and having a good time
while practicing their lines.

"Hey!" said Chrissy. "Let's put on some music, Barbara.
I know your sister's got a great collection of tapes."

Everyone was having so much fun that Barbara didn't
want to spoil the mood, but she knew that her older sister did
not like anyone to borrow her things without permission.

"I can't," she said.

"Why not?" said Stan. "Let's hear a few tunes."

Barbara knew that it would be a long time before her sister came home, and she might never know that Barbara had used her things. On the other hand, Barbara would feel terrible for going behind her back.

"My sister doesn't like me to use her stereo or tapes without her permission," said Barbara. "But I can turn on the radio."

"The radio?" said Orlando. "Forget it. Let's hear some of these tapes."

The kids started pressuring Barbara to take her sister's tapes.

"Come on, Barbara, don't be a spoilsport. We're not going to break anything," said Chrissy.

"I know that," said Barbara. "But rules are rules, and my sister trusts me. I'll bet there's some great music on the radio."

She switched the radio on and tuned it to her favorite station, and her friends soon stopped complaining. "Hey, that's not bad!" said Stan.

Later, when Barbara talked to her Dad about what had happened, he was very pleased that she had respected her

sister's wishes. "You did the right thing," he said. "That shows how grown-up you are, Barbara. And someone that grown-up deserves to have a few tapes of her own! I know you have a birthday coming up, and I think it's time that you had some special things for when your friends come over."

Barbara was happy, not just because soon she'd have her own tapes but because she hadn't been afraid to stand up for what was right.

What would you do if all your friends wanted you to do something that was wrong?

George's Story

A new kid moved onto George's block. He was very overweight and quiet, but every day he watched George and his friends, who were all ten and eleven years old, playing touch football in a vacant lot.

"I think he wants to join us," said Dale, one team's captain. "I don't want that fat kid on my team. Better ignore him."

Everyone said that they'd lose if they had this kid on their team, but George hated to see him standing at the fence, holding onto the iron grating and looking sad. The kid didn't have any friends.

"Get lost, fatso!" one of the boys yelled. He threw the football at the fence. Almost everyone laughed when the fat kid jumped back and fell down.

George didn't laugh. He couldn't get the kid's face out of his mind. He liked to win at football, but he didn't like hurting anyone. No matter what the other boys said, he was going to

invite the new kid to join them the very next day. Even if he didn't play football very well, he might be terrific at something else.

The next day George asked the new kid to play. His friends couldn't believe it when George walked over to the fence.

"What's your name?" George said to the new kid.

"George!" called Dale. "What're you doing?"

"I bet this guy can play a mean defense," George shouted back. He looked at the new boy and smiled.

"My name's Clinton," he said, smiling. He came around the fence and got into the game.

Clinton wasn't a very good football player—but he had an incredible sense of humor! He told jokes and made George, Dale, and the other boys laugh like crazy. George was glad he'd spoken up.

Have your friends ever teased someone? Have you?

Lucille's
Story

Lucille was having a birthday party to celebrate turning
eleven. Her family lived in a small apartment over a shoe
store, and there wasn't much room or light. But they had
hung purple and white party streamers all around to make the
place cheerful. Lucille's mother bought some flowers and
baked a huge cake. Her father had surprised Lucille with a
special package during breakfast—a brand new dress! It
promised to be a memorable day.

Lucille invited seven of her best friends to the party.
Everyone was having a good time. Lucille's Mom stepped
into the kitchen to put the finishing touches on the cake, and
Lucille's Dad ran out to the store for more soft drinks. As

soon as the adults' backs were turned, Emily pulled out a flask of bourbon.

"Now we can really have some fun," she said. A few of the other girls giggled and reached for the liquor.

"Hey! The birthday girl should get some," said Josephina. She held the flask under Lucille's nose.

Lucille didn't like the smell of alcohol at all. It smelled like fire. She also had seen the terrible things that her Uncle Martin did and said when he had been drinking, and she didn't think alcohol was much fun. The best way to keep it out of her life was never to start drinking.

"No," she said. "I don't need that stuff to celebrate."

"Loosen up!" said Emily. "It's your birthday!"

"That means I get to have whatever I want," Lucille said. "And I want us all to have a good time at my party without bourbon!"

"You won't get hooked with one drink," Josephina said.

"That sounds like the sort of thing my Uncle Martin always says," said Lucille. Just thinking of her uncle made her want to cry.

"Hey," said Emily. "You look upset, Lucille." She put the cap back on the flask.

Josephina reached over to pat Lucille's hand. "We want you to be happy on your birthday, Lucy," she said. "It's no big deal, O.K.? We're not going to ruin your party."

Lucille squeezed Josephina's hand. "Thanks," she said. "I'm glad you understand."

Then Lucille's mother brought out the cake, her father came back from the store, and the party continued. Lucille decided that later she would talk to her Dad about Uncle Martin, because she'd kept her sadness about him bottled up for too long. She also knew that even if Emily and Josephina didn't ask her to drink again, plenty of other kids would as she got older. Maybe her parents could suggest more ways for her to say no without losing her friends.

Has anyone ever offered you a drink? What did you do?

Jordan's Story

Some of Jordan's friends weren't doing too well in the sixth grade. They told Jordan that they would never get good jobs or be able to move out of the neighborhood, so why should they bother studying?

Jordan thought this was a silly attitude. They weren't giving themselves a chance! Jordan saw how hard his mother was working to put him through school. She'd only gone up to fourth grade herself, and then had quit to go to work. Jordan didn't know where his Dad was, and nobody was helping his mother support Jordan and his two brothers and baby sister.

It was his dream to show that he was worth something. He wanted to succeed for himself, and he very much wanted to make his mother proud. He didn't want her to have to work so hard.

A group of boys came to Jordan's house one afternoon when he was studying for a big exam. The Philadelphia Eagles football team was in town, practicing in a field only four miles away. Jordan's friends were going to go down there and peek through the fence.

Jordan was very tempted to go along. He loved football, and he didn't want these boys to think he was stuck-up. But this exam was important, and he needed to concentrate.

"Hey, Jordan, you work too hard!" said Carl.

"Come on, put that book down," Bill added.

"You know, Jordan, if you turn into too much of a brain, nobody's going to like you!" said Luke.

When Jordan heard that, he knew exactly what was happening. These boys didn't want him to do well on the exam. It embarrassed them to see someone getting ahead.

Who needed friends like that? He had high hopes for his future, and plenty of the kids at school thought he was fine the way he was. Some very smart and pretty girls in the Science Club wanted him to join, and the more Jordan listened to these boys, the better the girls' invitation sounded.

Jordan knew that the Eagles would be in town for a week. "I think we should go watch the Eagles tomorrow, to celebrate doing well on the exam," he said. "We can study together now, if you want." Jordan wanted to be nice and help his friends, but he wasn't going to sacrifice his own grades just because they were pressuring him!

"Forget it," said the boys. "We're getting out of here."

Jordan felt so terrible when they left that he discussed everything with his mother as soon as she came home from work.

"They just left you?" she said. "You must feel pretty terrible about that."

He nodded. "But when I thought about it, I realized that they only hang around me when they want me to do something."

"I'm glad you know Alan and Tyrone too," said his mother. "They're much better pals."

Jordan agreed. There were a lot of people out there who liked him for who he was. He decided that the very next day he would invite Alan and Tyrone to go watch the Eagles with him . . . right after he signed up for the Science Club!

What would you do?

Anita's
Story

Anita's friends talked about boys constantly. They never stopped! Anita liked some boys, but she thought there were plenty of other things to talk about.

Some of the girls wore lipstick and acted much older than they were. They bragged about kissing boys and running around with them. At every party, they wanted to play games like post office.

"Have you ever done anything like that, Anita?" Dolores asked.

Eugenia laughed. "Anita's blushing! She's blushing like a little baby!"

"It's time you started learning about boys, Anita," said Dolores. "Time to grow up!"

"If you want to hang around with us, Anita, you've got to get with it," Eugenia said.

Anita didn't know why Dolores and Eugenia were in such a hurry to grow up. What she *did* know was that she didn't want to be pressured into doing anything with boys until she

was ready. In fact, she thought Dolores and Eugenia sounded a little ridiculous.

"You'll have to like me the way I am," said Anita. "I have plenty of time for boys and dating when I'm older!"

That night she talked to her mother. She still felt a little bad that the girls had laughed at her.

"I know you're upset," said her mother, "but don't let anybody push you into anything you don't want to do."

"Do you think they'll still be my friends?" asked Anita.

"I think so," her mother said. "You have many things in common. And you have plenty of other friends who are very mature and popular and who don't tease you about boys."

Anita realized that was true. She shouldn't let Dolores and Eugenia get to her. She had lots of great friends, including boys, and she would think about dating when she was ready.

How would you feel if your friends teased you?

Abe's
Story

Abe liked hanging around with his old pal, Joe. They spent many Saturday afternoons together, and now that Joe's parents were divorced, the boys often spent their evenings together too. Joe hated going home, because sometimes his mother drank too much and yelled at him. Abe was twelve and Joe was ten, so Abe felt a little protective of his friend.

One day, while they were sitting together doing their homework, Joe turned to Abe and said, "You know that woman my Dad is seeing now? The one who lives on Delmore Avenue?"

Abe nodded. Joe had a funny expression on his face, and Abe was worried. "What about her?" he asked.

Joe reached into his book pack and pulled out a can of spray paint. "She's always telling my Dad how much she wants to redecorate her house. Well, you and I are going to help her!"

"You want to spray paint her house?" said Abe.

"That's right," said Joe, "but you've got to help me." Joe began talking about the nasty things he wanted to write on the woman's garage.

Abe felt terrible. "I can't do that, Joe. Come on. You should forget about it."

"What kind of a friend are you?" asked Joe. "I can't believe you won't help me."

Abe knew that Joe was very upset about his parents' divorce, but this seemed like a bad way to handle it. "Spray painting her house won't change anything, Joe," he said.

Joe threw the can of paint at Abe, but didn't hit him. "I dare you," he said. "If you don't, I'm leaving right now, and I won't talk to you ever again."

Abe was very upset. Joe was his best friend, and they'd been pals for so long that Abe couldn't imagine being without him. He picked up the can of paint. He knew that they could run over to Delmore Avenue, write something on the woman's wall, and disappear in an instant. They probably wouldn't get caught, and Joe would be happy.

"I dare you," Joe said again.

Suddenly Abe realized that since he and Joe were such good friends, they should be able to talk this over. He

remembered that his parents had taught him that when someone dared him to do something, he should ask *why*.

"Why do you want to do this, Joe?" asked Abe.

Joe put his head in his hands. He started to cry. "I don't know," he said. "I hate having my Dad gone."

Abe put his arm around his friend. "Maybe you should talk to your Dad and tell him how much you miss him," he said, "and maybe there's a counselor at school who can talk to you. Plus you know that you can always talk to me!"

Joe nodded. He and Abe talked for a while, and then Joe went home. Abe threw away the can of spray paint.

What would you do if someone dared you to do something that you knew was wrong?

Rachel's
Story

Rachel's father owned a 7-11 store, and sometimes she would go there after school and help with little things. She'd stack the candies or ice cream bars, or dust the counter.

One day some girls a little older than Rachel, who was ten, started talking to her at school. Rachel thought she was walking on air! These were the prettiest, most popular girls in the whole school, and they had picked her as a friend!

Rachel invited them to come to the store so that they could all have an ice cream together.

When the girls came by, they asked Rachel to come outside.

"Steal some wine and beer for us, Rachel," said Carol.

Rachel was shocked. Then she noticed that the girls had funny smiles on their faces, as if they had already been drinking. She smelled alcohol on their breath.

Rachel was angry that these girls had made friends with her just because they thought she could get them some free beer. She didn't care how big they were at school; she would never be their little thief!

"No," she said. "You'd better leave right now." The girls realized Rachel wouldn't help them, so they left. Rachel went inside and told her father what had happened.

"I'm glad you came and told me, Rachel," her Dad said. "I know you wanted those girls to like you, but you have so many nice friends, who would never ask you to steal for them. I'm happy you didn't let yourself be pushed around."

"So am I, Dad," said Rachel.

What would you do?

Conrad's Story

Conrad adored his older brother, Mike. Mike was a wonderful pianist and a great athlete, and a good friend. If he was planning to do something fun, he would often ask Conrad to join in, even though he was fifteen and Conrad was only ten. Not many older brothers were like that! As far as Conrad was concerned, everything that Mike said and did was perfect.

One weekend Mike and his friends Stuart and Jim took Conrad to Marine Park. They were all having a great time until Stuart pulled out some dope. "Let's get high," he said.

"Do you think we should?" asked Mike. He looked a little nervous.

Conrad was very upset. Who would be stupid enough to take drugs when there were so many wonderful dolphins and fish to enjoy at Marine Park? Why didn't Mike just say no? Conrad knew that the best thing to do around drugs was to walk away immediately and tell his parents what had happened, but he didn't want to leave his brother!

Jim saw the expression on Conrad's face. "What's the matter, little brother? Afraid we won't share it with you?" He laughed.

When Mike heard that, he spoke up at once. "Leave him alone, you guys! He's right."

"Aw, come on, Mike. Don't tell me you're a chicken too!" said Stuart.

Mike put his arm around Conrad, and that made Conrad feel great. He had been afraid of being all alone against these bigger boys, and he was glad that Mike was standing up to them.

"Conrad and I are going to enjoy the park without that stuff," said Mike. "We've got better things to do."

"O.K., take it easy," said Stuart. "I'll get rid of it."

"Good," said Mike.

Conrad thought Mike was not only a great big brother, he was a wonderful example.

What would you do if someone offered you dope?

Joanne's
Story

Twelve-year-old Joanne was very excited about the piano recital coming up. She had practiced the "Moonlight Sonata" over and over until she knew it perfectly. Her teacher, Mrs. Johnson, was pleased because Joanne was going to receive a special award after the recital. Joanne's parents told her how proud they were. They took her out for a special dinner, along with Lawrence, her older brother, and Christina, her younger sister.

Everything was going fine until Margaret, one of Joanne's friends from piano class, came up to her and said,

"You know, Joanne, everyone's mad because you're getting that award tomorrow night. It's not fair! We work as hard as you do. If you want to stay friends with us, you'd better mess up a little. Nobody likes a girl who's perfect!"

Joanne was extremely upset. She wanted the girls to like her. She helped them with their music whenever they asked, without trying to act like their teacher. She never gloated about her playing—if anything, she was shy about it! Yet she wanted to do her best.

She decided to talk to her parents.

"Joanne, why do you think Margaret said those things?" asked her father.

Joanne thought for a moment. "I don't know," she said. "Maybe they think I'm showing off."

"Are you?" said her father.

"No!" said Joanne. "I just do my best!"

"Do you think they might be jealous of you?" asked her mother.

"I'll bet they are," chimed in Lawrence. "Don't let them get to you, Joanne."

"But they're my friends," Joanne said. She felt like crying.

"Tell you what," her father said. "I have an idea. Why don't we talk to Mrs. Johnson about getting you into the more advanced class? That way you'll be around people who play as well as you do."

Joanne thought that this sounded like a good idea, but she wasn't sure. At the recital the next day, she played "Moonlight Sonata" as well as she could. It felt great! Afterward a girl named Courtney, who was in Mrs. Johnson's advanced class, came up to her and said, "Joanne, I hear you might be joining us soon. I'm so glad! I loved hearing you play tonight. We'll have a lot in common."

Courtney sat down with Joanne and they talked about music for a while. Then Joanne's family rushed up to give her a big hug and congratulate her on her performance. Joanne felt like she was on top of the world! If she'd given in to the pressure from Margaret not to do well, she would be feeling miserable—and there would be no guarantee those girls

would like her any better. She was glad she'd talked the whole thing over with her parents, and she was especially glad to have met Courtney.

What would you do if someone was pressuring you to fail?

Andre's Story

Andre had been in a wheelchair for four years, ever since he'd been in a car accident when he was six years old. Sometimes people stared at him in a way that made him uncomfortable, but he told himself that they didn't mean any harm. They were only curious. He loved to paint and read. He also loved going fishing with his friend Chris and Chris's father.

One day Chris and two other boys came to see Andre. They wanted to go to the boardwalk at the beach, but their parents wouldn't let them. Some pretty rough people hung around there.

"You've got to help us out, Andre," Chris said. "We told our parents that we're studying with you."

"That's right," said Michael. "If they call, say we're in the shower or something." He laughed.

Andre thought of all the wonderful times he'd spent with Chris. Not just fishing by the lake, but other good times, too.

Andre didn't expect Chris to include him in every single trip or plan, but how could Chris ask him to lie?

"It's no big deal," said Chris, seeing Andre hesitate.

Andre did not have many friends besides Chris, and the thought of losing him was terrifying. But he would never forgive himself if something happened to Chris because he'd been afraid to speak up. "It *is* a big deal, Chris. I can't lie for you," he said. "It would be terrible if something went wrong."

"Come on, don't be a jerk," Michael said.

Chris could see how unhappy Andre was, and he felt bad that he and these boys were putting so much pressure on Andre.

"Leave him alone," Chris said to the other boys. "He's right. What if something did happen to us?"

Andre was pleased to hear Chris stand up for him. Instead of having a fight, their little disagreement had actually made them even better friends!

What would you say if someone asked you to lie?